ANIMALS ON THE MOVE

BY LAND

WRITTEN BY
Eliza Nodes

PowerKiDS press

Published in 2026
by The Rosen Publishing Group, Inc.
2544 Clinton Street, Buffalo, NY 14224

Written by: Eliza Nodes
Edited by: Rebecca Phillips-Bartlett
Designed by: Rob Delph

All facts, statistics, web addresses, and URLs in this book were verified as valid and accurate at time of writing. No responsibility for any changes to external websites or references can be accepted by either the author or publisher.

Cataloging-in-Publication Data

Names: Nodes, Eliza.

Title: By land / Eliza Nodes.

Description: Buffalo, New York : PowerKids Press, 2026. | Series: Animals on the move | Includes glossary and index.

Identifiers: ISBN 9781499455779 (pbk.) | ISBN 9781499455786 (library bound) | ISBN 9781499455793 (ebook)

Subjects: LCSH: Animal migration--Juvenile literature. | Animal behavior--Juvenile literature. | Adaption--Juvenile literature.

Classification: LCC QL754.N634 2026 | DDC 591.568--dc23

Printed in China

CPSIA Compliance Information: Batch #QW26PK. For further information contact Rosen Publishing at 1-800-237-9932.

PHOTO CREDITS

All images are courtesy of Shutterstock.com, unless otherwise stated. Front Cover – Neil Bowman, Rudmer Zwerver, longtaildog, GUDKOV ANDREY. 2&3 – Mark Time Author, Sergey Krasnoshchokov. 4&5 – muratart, Jenny_Vi, TheLearningPhotographer, KensCanning. 6&7 – Mcknub, TUBS, CC BY-SA 3.0 <https://creativecommons.org/licenses/by-sa/3.0>, via Wikimedia Commons, TUBS, CC BY-SA 3.0 <https://creativecommons.org/licenses/by-sa/3.0>, via Wikimedia Commons, alvarog1970. 8&9 – Roger de la Harpe, Harry Collins Photography, GUDKOV ANDREY. 10&11 – Mark Time Author, TUBS, CC BY-SA 3.0 <https://creativecommons.org/licenses/by-sa/3.0>, via Wikimedia Commons, S B Stock. 12&13 – Neil Bowman, David Stanley from Nanaimo, Canada, CC BY 2.0 <https://creativecommons.org/licenses/by/2.0>, via Wikimedia Commons, Sofia Varano. 14&15 – tunasalmon, Tom Reichner, Nick Fox. 16&17 – Ian Dewar Photography, Richard Seeley, Kit Leong. 18&19 – Harbin, Public domain, via Wikimedia Commons, Katpatuka (talk · contribs), FAL, via Wikimedia Commons, Sergey Krasnoshchokov, blutack. 20&21 – Jukka Jantunen, Vladimir Melnikov. 22&23 – Roman Samborskyi, Roman Samborskyi, abubakar0023, Mr_Karesuando, Subhamay Acharyya, Bohdan Populov.

CONTENTS

Words that look like this can be found in the glossary on page 24.

WHAT IS MIGRATION?

Migration is the movement of animals from one place to another. Many animals, including birds and insects, migrate every year. Some animals migrate more than once a year. Other animals are always on the move.

Animals migrate for lots of reasons, such as:

- To find food and water
- To find somewhere to have young
- To avoid challenging weather
- Because of changes to their habitat

Let's look at some land animals that migrate.

THE WILDEBEEST'S GREAT MIGRATION

Africa's Great Migration is the largest group migration on Earth. Two million animals take part in the Great Migration. Over a million of these animals are wildebeest. They make this journey alongside zebras and gazelles.

The wildebeest herd is so big you can see it from space!

The wildebeest herd travels from northern Tanzania to southern Kenya and back again. They move in this circle throughout the year. The wildebeest can walk up to 620 miles (1,000 km) on this journey.

Wildebeest are herbivores, which means they only eat plants. They migrate to find fresh grass to eat. Rain helps the grass grow, so they follow the rainfall from Tanzania to Kenya.

The Great Migration is a dangerous journey. There are many wide rivers and predators, such as crocodiles, along the way. Staying in large groups helps the wildebeest stay safe on their journey to greener grasslands.

What animal is this?

THE CHRISTMAS ISLAND RED CRAB'S QUEST

The Christmas Island red crab lives on Australia's Christmas Island. During the rainy season, from November to January, over 100 million crabs scurry onto the island's roads and beaches.

Christmas Island red crabs make a yearly migration from the rainforest to the ocean. This is so the female crabs can lay their eggs. One female can lay up to 100,000 eggs!

How many crabs can you see on the beach?

To help the crabs make their way safely, people have built bridges over busy roads. There are road signs, roads are sometimes closed, and the radio announces migration updates.

When the male crabs arrive at the ocean, they dig burrows. The female crabs join them in the burrows to mate. After two weeks in the burrows, the female crabs release their eggs into the ocean. Then, they return to the rainforest.

young Christmas Island red crabs

THE AMERICAN BISON PLOWS ON

American bison, or plains bison, live in North America. They mostly live on the Northern Great Plains. This stretches across parts of the United States and Canada.

In the 1800s, American bison nearly became extinct. This was because humans hunted them and forced them to leave their grassland habitats. Since then, bison numbers have risen because they are protected.

Protected means they are kept safe by rules humans made.

American bison travel in large herds. They usually migrate in a loop, walking hundreds of miles. They migrate to find more food, especially during the winter.

Bison use their heads as snowplows to clear thick snow on top of grass.

American bison are grazers, which means they eat grass and other plants. When they have finished grazing, more sunlight can reach the plants. This means the plants are healthier for other animals to eat.

THE CARIBOU'S ARCTIC TREK

Caribou is another name for reindeer. They are known as caribou in North America. Caribou come from Alaska, but herds can be found across the Arctic tundra.

The caribou has the longest migration of any land animal.

Caribou migrate in large herds to protect themselves from predators. They let others know if there is any danger. Caribou's ankles crack as they walk. This means they can hear if the herd starts to run.

Caribou walk over 1,240 miles (2,000 km) every year.

Caribou migrate across the Arctic tundra for food and to protect their young from predators. When they have young, female caribou need more food so they can keep making milk for them.

Caribou are affected by climate change. Climate change causes more rain. The rain freezes the grass, making it too icy for the caribou to eat. They can use their hooves to clear snow but not ice.

"Caribou" is a French-Canadian word. It means "pawer" or "scratcher."

WHAT HAVE YOU LEARNED?

Let's see what you can remember about these land animals that migrate. It is time for a quiz! Get your paper and pencil ready to write down your answers!

QUESTIONS

1. Why do wildebeest migrate?

2. Name one thing people have done to help Christmas Island red crabs.

3. What part of their bodies do American bison use to clear snow off the ground?

4. How do caribou protect themselves from predators?

Answers:

1. To find grass to eat
2. Built bridges; closed roads; put up road signs; made radio updates
3. Heads
4. By traveling in large groups

GLOSSARY

CLIMATE CHANGE	a change in the typical weather or temperature of a large area
EXTINCT	when an animal no longer exists
HABITAT	the natural home in which animals, plants, and other living things live
HERD	a group of animals that live together
MATE	to produce young with an animal of the same species
PREDATORS	animals that hunt other animals for food
TUNDRA	a cold and treeless area in the Arctic
UPDATES	things that make something more up-to-date

INDEX